The Dust Bowl

by Elaina Jacobs

TABLE OF CONTENTS

Introduction

In the 1930s, the Great **Plains** of the United States experienced a period of **devastating** dust storms. Fierce winds blew dirt and debris through the air, blocking out the sun and turning day into night. Swirling black clouds of dust moved across the land, blanketing everything in their path. People walking outside had to cover their faces with wet rags to keep the dust out of their eyes and nostrils. They ran for shelter and waited for the dust to settle.

The center of the Dust Bowl stretched into five states.

N
W E
S

Denver, Colorado

Topeka, Kansas

Santa Fe, New Mexico

Oklahoma City, Oklahoma

Austin, Texas

Even indoors, it was hard to escape the dust. Dirt blew through cracks in the walls and filtered down from the ceiling.

Each dust storm was a nightmare that lasted for hours. And the storms raged for eight long years. People lived in constant fear of when the next big storm might hit. It could be tomorrow, next week, or next month. The storms were unpredictable, and it seemed like nothing could be done to stop them.

This was life in the Dust Bowl.

CHAPTER 1

The Great Plains

The first people to live on the windy Great Plains were Native Americans. They grew squash, corn, and beans, and supplemented their diets with wild game, such as bison. Rainfall was unpredictable, however, and some years yielded few crops.

The landscape in the southern plains was lush an green, and the soil was rich. A thick blanket of buffa grass spread across the land and held the soil in plac Even in tough conditions, such as heat or **drought**, the buffalo grass survived and kept the soil fertile.

In the 1850s, European settlers flocked to the southern Great Plains to farm. There was plenty of cheap land on which to grow corn and wheat and raise cattle. The farmers had experienced success before in the East, and they continued to farm as they always had. The sod in the southern plains was hard, but a new, strong steel plow had been invented, and farmers used horses and mules to pull the plows through fields and break up the soil.

The dominant crop in the Great Plains was wheat.

EYEWITNESS REPORT

"There's nothin' like this country when it rains, I mean as far as the grassland is beautiful, the Brahma grass and buffalo grass. With rain, the country produces something as good as nearly anywhere in the world, because we have a variety of soil. We have the black land, tight lands, sandy land, and the mix, you see. So it's—it's a wonderful country."

—Melt White, Dust Bowl survivor

Buffalo grass got its name from the herds of buffalo, or bison, that used it as their main source of food.

Farming Expands

Then in 1920, farmers in the southern plains began using tractors, gradually replacing their horses and mules. With tractors, more land could be plowed, and the farmers could plant more crops.

The growth of railroad transportation also gave farmers an easy way to transport products to customers in other parts of the country. High demand for bread in the East quickly made wheat the most popular crop. Wheat prices soared to an all-time high of two dollars per **bushel**.

These rising prices led many farmers to believe they could build their own fortune with wheat crops. More and more farmers moved onto the southern plains, bought land, and planted wheat. Despite the droughts that had once occurred in the region, abundant rains helped the wheat crops grow.

Some people who came to the southern Great Plains didn't know much about farming but believed that this vast area of farmland was profitable. They wanted a way to get rich quickly and thought farming was the solution to their economic woes. These "suitcase farmers," as they were called, also plowed the lands.

Because of all the plowing that occurred during this time—more than five million acres of grasslands had been turned into wheat fields—the period became known as "the great plow-up." By early 1930, tall stalks of wheat grew where the green expanse of buffalo grasses had once covered the land. This land was later abandoned by these opportunistic "suitcase farmers" when the price of produce, grain, and other staples fell dramatically during the Great Depression.

With the arrival of tractors, land that had been reserved for supporting animals could now be plowed for cash crops.

EYEWITNESS REPORT

When the stock market crashed and the Great Depression began, the price of staple crops fell drastically. As a result, the "suitcase farmers," whose only stake in cultivating land in the Great Plains was to reap profits, simply vacated their land, leaving behind large stretches of barren farmland. The land was now vulnerable to the elements and at great risk of becoming wholly infertile.

"That's kindly a human trait: we don't think. We don't think, except for ourselves and it comes down to greed. You know, we're selfish and we want—we're self-centered and we want what we want and we don't even think of what the end results might be."

—Melt White, Dust Bowl survivor

CHAPTER 2

The Great Depression Begins

The 1920s were a time of prosperity for many Americans. After the end of World War I, the country was filled with a sense of **optimism** about the future. Positive attitudes led many Americans to spend more money. One way people spent their money was by investing it in the stock market. Stories spread about investors making big fortunes in the market, and soon more and more people wanted to invest.

But the booming stock market that so many people had begun to rely on would soon be the cause of their biggest economic trials. On October 29, 1929, the United States stock market crashed, and most stocks became worthless. As a result of this disaster, many banks failed and went bankrupt, companies closed, and people lost their jobs.

RISKY INVESTMENTS

Although the stock market was a risky investment, even for the wealthiest investors, many people thought the possibility of success outweighed any risks. Even those who couldn't afford to buy stocks chose to invest and bought stocks "on margin." With this loan system, they could pay for a small portion of the stock prices and then borrow the rest. The stock market became so popular that banks even began to use their customers' money to invest in the market without the customers knowing.

The United States entered what would be known as the Great Depression. With fifteen million people out of work, the economy suffered. Most people did not have any money to spend and so prices dropped. Wheat that once cost two dollars per bushel was down to forty cents.

The farmers in the southern plains saw only one solution: plant more wheat. These farmers hoped wheat would be a bumper crop, or a crop that yields an unusually large harvest. The idea was that the fertile land of the Great Plains would help them sell an abnormally large amount of wheat, which would then cover the monetary deficit created by the price drop. In other words, they would sell more wheat at a lower price, rather than less wheat at a higher price. Unfortunately, the more wheat they planted, the fewer grasslands were left on the plains.

EYEWITNESS REPORT

"The Depression actually started in '29. That's when that stock market and everything went. Then everything dropped. Corn, I seen on the board in Hampton—that's where we lived at that time when it started—nine cents a bushel. . . . And, everything just went all to pieces. Eggs was ten cents a dozen. And your wheat, I really don't know just what the wheat did, dropped too."

—LeRoy Hankel, Dust Bowl survivor

CHAPTER 3

The Dust Storms

After wheat prices dropped, many of the people who came seeking easy money left the southern Great Plains. The large stretches of land that had once been lush grasslands and then wheat crops were now bare and open. Too many cattle had overgrazed on the grassland. Farmers had overplowed the land and used farming **techniques** more suited to rainy climates.

In 1930, the rains stopped, and a drought hit the Great Plains. The lack of rain prevented crop growth and caused the wheat fields to dry up. Yet the winds raged on as they always had. With no roots to hold down the soil, the wind picked up the loose dirt and carried it along, creating dust storms called "black blizzards."

Fourteen of these blizzards would blow through the region in 1932, and that number would more than double the following year, with thirty-eight storms in 1933.

ELECTRICITY IN THE AIR

During dust storms, the air became charged with static electricity. People would not shake hands for fear of sparks passing between them. Automobiles shorted out and would not run. Modern science has been able to discern that the enormous amount of static electricity was a result of two things: the dry air prevalent in the Great Plains and the collision of dust particles.

When dust particles collide, the smaller particles steal electrons from the larger particles, flipping their respective charges: smaller particles become negative, while larger particles become positive. When the winds carry the smaller particles into the air, the separation between them and the larger particles creates an electrical field, the origin of the static electricity.

In Lankin, Kansas, 1935, three children leave for school wearing goggles and homemade dust masks.

During the dust storms, schools were often closed. Sometimes, though, the storms started after schools were already in session and children got stuck in their classrooms. Schoolteachers lit lanterns so the students could read and write. On some days, the teachers kept their students at the schoolhouse until the storm was over, and occasionally this meant they had to stay overnight! Since walking home during a dust storm could have been deadly, teachers had to do what they could to keep the children safe.

Despite the harsh and unforgiving conditions of the Dust Bowl, only one out of every four farmers decided to migrate to another part of the country. Unfortunately, it was extremely difficult to find a new place that provided the opportunity to make a living. Of the 2.5 million people who attempted to leave the Great Plains by 1940, 200,000 tried to migrate to California. Many of these people were turned away as "undesirables." Even those who managed to cross the border found themselves taking the jobs of migrant workers, picking grapes and cotton. Many were forced to give up farming because the land was owned by corporations. Still, some bought small plots of land and put together shack homes with scraps of wood and other materials they found lying about.

EYEWITNESS REPORT

"One day in March 1934, my beginners were busy reading. All of a sudden there was total darkness. It was as though a huge curtain had been drawn around our building. . . . I realized a dust storm had hit because soon the room was filled with a 'fog of dust.' . . . We teachers walked home holding wet towels over our faces in order to breathe."

—schoolteacher Taleta Elfeldt, from *Telling Tales Out of School*

Covered in Dust

The aftermath of a dust storm was as **grueling** as the storm itself. People had to wrench themselves free from heavy dirt and debris, which was no easy task. Equipment was submerged in sand, and barns and sheds were sheathed in mounds of dirt.

Despite the fact that people had sealed up their homes and covered any openings, the dust still seeped through the cracks. Floors were covered with inches of dirt. Dishes had to be washed. Sheets and clothes had to be taken outside and shaken and later washed.

Very often, repairs would be made, homes would be scrubbed clean, and clothes would be washed just before another storm would blow through and cover everything with dirt again.

A deep layer of **grit** constantly coated nearly every surface and made its way into people's mouths, noses, and ears. Many people even suffered from a lung condition called "dust pneumonia" because the dust had settled in their lungs.

There was no escaping the dust. By 1934, the southern plains had been transformed into little more than a desert.

EYEWITNESS REPORT

"The impact is like a shovelful of fine sand flung against the face. People caught in their own yards grope for the doorstep. Cars come to a standstill, for no light in the world can penetrate that swirling murk. . . . We live with the dust, eat it, sleep with it, watch it strip us of possessions and the hope of possessions. It is becoming Real."

—Avis D. Carlson, writing in the *New Republic*

A Record-Setting
DROUGHT

The 1930s drought was one of the longest in American history, and the somber and hopeless mood of the times was made even worse by the onset of the Great Depression.

The year 1934 was an especially dry year, with more than 75 percent of the country under drought conditions.

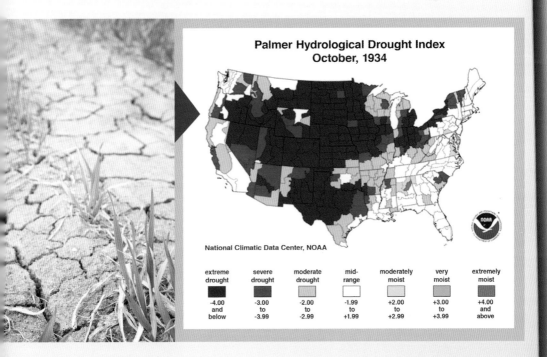

Palmer Hydrological Drought Index
October, 1934

National Climatic Data Center, NOAA

extreme drought	severe drought	moderate drought	mid-range	moderately moist	very moist	extremely moist
-4.00 and below	-3.00 to -3.99	-2.00 to -2.99	-1.99 to +1.99	+2.00 to +2.99	+3.00 to +3.99	+4.00 and above

Scientists today can use modern equipment to predict weather patterns and give people information about how long bad weather conditions will last. In the 1930s, though, this equipment was not available. People suffering through the drought had to go through each day not knowing when rain might come again. It was a trying time for many Americans.

CHAPTER 4

Black Sunday

Because of the severe drought affecting much of the United States, 1934 was a particularly devastating year. The "Yearbook of Agriculture" reported that millions of acres of land had lost their topsoil. And dust storms blew from the Great Plains into other parts of the country. Yet, somehow, the worst conditions were still to be seen.

On April 14, 1935, the Great Plains would face its worst storm yet.

After several weeks of dust storms, the weather had finally become more pleasant. April 14 began as a sunny spring Sunday, and families went outside to enjoy the warm weather. However, in the afternoon, ferocious winds began to blow in eastern and northeastern Oklahoma. And then the storm spread to southern Oklahoma and Texas.

This storm was different from the previous storms, which were caused by warmer winds blowing from the south. Masses of cold air had traveled south from Canada, and the heavier cold air pushed away the warm air, causing high winds to blow from 65 to 95 kilometers (about 40 to 60 miles) per hour.

EYEWITNESS REPORT

"Severe dust storm hit at 4:20 P.M., turning afternoon brightness immediately into midnight darkness, and absolutely zero visibility. . . . The storm came from the north and northeast and traveled at a very great speed."

—Ralph H. Guy, weather observer in Kenton, Oklahoma

The wind churned up the soil, creating walls of dirt more than 2,400 meters (about 8,000 feet) high. Thunder boomed and lightning cracked through the sky, but no rain fell. The sky turned black, and a wall of dust blocked out the sun. To some, it must have seemed like the end of the world.

First-person accounts from witnesses of the storm described a huge black cloud approaching, and quickly. As the storm raged through, it pushed mounds of dirt into houses and coated everything. The thick black dust made it impossible to see anything. Anyone out on the street frantically sought shelter. They ran for whatever cover they could find and then sat in terror for hours, waiting for the dust to pass.

Widespread damage was left behind in the wake of this "Black Sunday."

EYEWITNESS REPORTS

"There was absolutely no light. . . . I got down and I thought I could see, but there was the highway around the place and I was afraid I'd be walkin' out on the highway. Well, I got down and looked, put my nose to the ground, seen no more light. It was totally just like being in a salt mine or a coal mine."

—Clayton Hall, from the Dust Bowl Oral History Project

"It was as though the sky was divided into two opposite worlds. On the south there was blue sky, golden sunlight and tranquility; on the north, there was a menacing curtain of boiling black dust that appeared to reach a thousand or more feet into the air. It had the appearance of a mammoth waterfall in reverse—color as well as form. . . . We were stunned. Never had we been in such all-enveloping blackness before, such impenetrable gloom."

—Pauline Winkler Grey, *The Black Sunday of April 14, 1935* (Kansas Historical Society)

"A great black bank rolled in out of the northeast, and in a twinkling when it struck Liberal, plunged everything into inky blackness, worse than that on any midnight, when there is at least some starlight and outlines of objects can be seen. When the storm struck it was impossible to see one's hand before his face even two inches away. And it was several minutes before any trace of daylight whatsoever returned."

—*Liberal News*, April 15, 1935, Kansas

Reporter Robert Geiger was in the southern Great Plains on that fateful Sunday, and his account of the devastation was included in the *Lubbock Evening Journal* (Texas) the next day. In his article, he referred to the region as the "dust bowl." This nickname quickly spread and became a popular term used by newspapers, speechmakers, and government officials.

CHAPTER 5

Westward Migration

The combination of the dust storms and the Great Depression had devastating effects on the people of the Great Plains. Hundreds of thousands of people could no longer afford their homes and were left homeless. After years of failed crops and ruined farms, many farmers abandoned their land and took to the road. Tales of wealth and "streets paved with gold" in California filtered throughout the Dust Bowl, and those who could packed up their cars and left the region.

This migration away from the Plains states was the largest migration in American history. One quarter of the population from the region—more than two million people—left during this time, and about 200,000 of them ended up in California.

Many Californians resented the refugees from the Great Plains and referred to them as "Okies," a nickname for people from Oklahoma, even if they were from other states.

NEXT TIME TRY THE TRAIN
RELAX Southern Pacific

But life in California was also full of hardships. Many **refugees** from the Great Plains were reduced to becoming migrant workers, people who move from place to place to harvest crops. Not only was migrant work hard and tiring, it also paid barely adequate wages. Most of the farms in California were run by corporations, and in many situations, the farms hired more workers than they needed and then paid each person less money.

Migrant workers were often forced to live in tent camps or other community housing. Other people, not wanting to work for the corporate farms, set up their own towns on open lots they were able to purchase cheaply. They put together meager shacks and lived without **amenities**, such as plumbing and electricity. Poor conditions in these places led to widespread illness and disease.

The Dust Bowl era was documented in many ways. Artists, musicians, and writers were moved to capture the times.

Dorothea Lange

Dorothea Lange worked as a portrait photographer in California before she began taking pictures for the Resettlement Administration, an agency that helped families relocate. During the Great Depression, she captured many images of people in difficult times, including the migrant workers displaced from the Dust Bowl.

One of her photographs, called *Migrant Mother*, is perhaps the most iconic image of the Dust Bowl. The photo, taken in 1936 in California, shows a distraught Florence Owens Thompson along with her children. At the time the picture was taken, Thompson was thirty-two years old and told Lange that she had just sold the tires from her car in order to buy food.

Resettled Farm Child, New Mexico, 1935

Toward Los Angeles, California, 1937

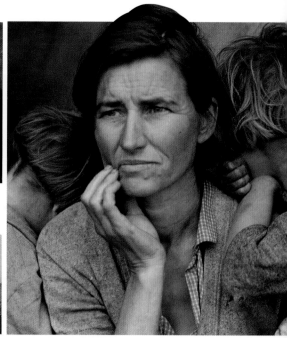

Migrant Mother, 1936

Woody Guthrie

Woody Guthrie was a popular folksinger who lived through the Dust Bowl, traveled with migrant workers, and wrote songs about their experiences. One song he wrote was "Dust Bowl Blues," about a farmer who loses his farm to the dust. It is speculated that the song is referring, in particular, to the Black Sunday dust storm. Later, Guthrie would write "This Land Is Your Land," one of the most popular songs about the United States.

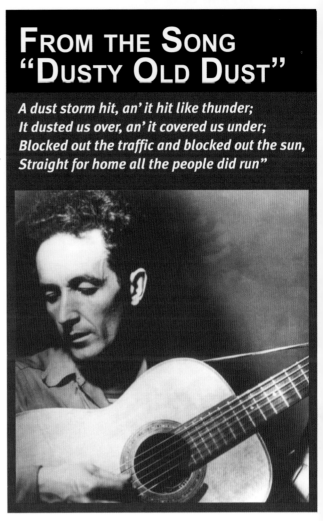

FROM THE SONG "DUSTY OLD DUST"

A dust storm hit, an' it hit like thunder;
It dusted us over, an' it covered us under;
Blocked out the traffic and blocked out the sun,
Straight for home all the people did run"

John Steinbeck

John Steinbeck was a writer from Salinas, California. He wrote several novels set in the Dust Bowl. One of Steinbeck's most famous works is the Pulitzer Prize–winning *The Grapes of Wrath*, published in 1939. It tells the story of a migrant family that leaves the Dust Bowl to work in California. The hardships experienced by the novel's Joad family are realistic portrayals of what many refugee families faced during these times. The novel opened many Americans' eyes to the **plight** of the migrant workers.

CHAPTER 6

The Need for Change

The 1930s were a difficult time for most Americans, not only those living in the Great Plains. People were tired of suffering and demanded change. When the newly elected president, Franklin D. Roosevelt, took office in 1933, people had high hopes that he would help restore the country to its prior state of prosperity.

Indeed, Roosevelt did have bold ideas about how to repair the shattered economy and improve conditions in the country. He felt that the government should directly help the American people, and he vowed that it would do so with his "New Deal" plan. Immediately after Roosevelt took office, he began implementing new bills aimed at improving conditions in the country.

EYEWITNESS REPORTS

"I see one-third of the nation ill-housed, ill-clad, ill-nourished. . . . The test of our progress is not whether we add more to the abundance of those who have much; it is whether we provide enough for those who have too little."
—Franklin D. Roosevelt, 1937

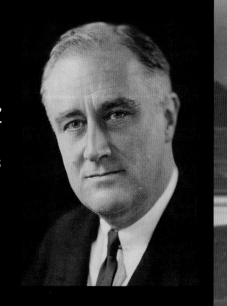

Although the president's focus was on helping the whole country, one of his advisers, Hugh H. Bennett, was particularly interested in addressing the problems in the Dust Bowl. As an educated farmer and the director of the newly created Soil Erosion Service, Bennett hoped to inform others about the best ways of farming. He criticized the overplowing that helped create the Dust Bowl and called for massive **reform** of farming techniques.

One day when Bennett was in Washington talking to Congress about the need for soil conservation, dirt from a large dust storm blew into the city. The fact that the spreading dust had reached that far east was strong evidence for Bennett's case. Later in 1935, Congress passed the Soil Conservation Act.

In March 1935, a dust storm blew from the Midwest all the way to the East Coast. It blackened the sky in Washington, D.C., as seen in this photo of the Lincoln Memorial.

Under this act, the government helped farmers institute better agricultural practices. Bennett showed farmers how to rotate their crops instead of planting the same crop in the same place year after year. He introduced contour plowing, which involves plowing in curves instead of straight lines. He also showed farmers how to plant cover crops, which are crops that stop erosion and replenish the soil with nutrients.

THE ROAD TO RECOVERY

In 1935, President Roosevelt approved $525 million to help people recover from the widespread drought. He also established the Works Progress Administration, or WPA, and put people back to work.

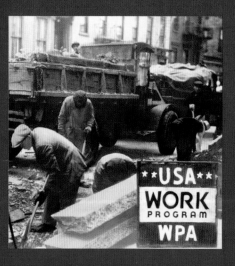

The government also helped the Plains states recover from the damage of the dust storms by planting trees and new grass, which would hold the soil down.

These efforts had a significant impact on the Great Plains. The dust storms were drastically reduced, and people began the process of recovery.

In 1939, the rains finally returned. And between the wet weather and the start of World War II, the price of produce increased as dramatically as it had fallen at the start of the Great Depression. It was not long before the Plains became a source of prosperity again.

A car parked in front of a sand drift during the Dust Bowl era.

The same car parked in the same location in 1941, after the Soil Conservation Act.

Conclusion

Although another drought hit the area in the 1950s, the land was able to withstand the dry conditions. The new farming practices instituted by the Roosevelt administration after the Dust Bowl helped preserve the land. The grasslands, laden with replanted trees, grass, and other vegetation, held the soil in place during high winds.

About this time, farmers also discovered a huge aquifer, or underground lake, that spread from Nebraska to Texas. They tapped this water and began pumping it up to the ground's surface to irrigate the land. They began planting crops that require more water, like corn.

Today farms in the southern Great Plains produce much of the food we find in our grocery stores. However, one nagging question is: What will happen when the aquifer is exhausted? For now it remains vast but it is gradually being depleted. Time will tell if the farmers have learned from the mistakes of the 1930s, and if they have done all they can to preserve the area known as "America's Heartland."

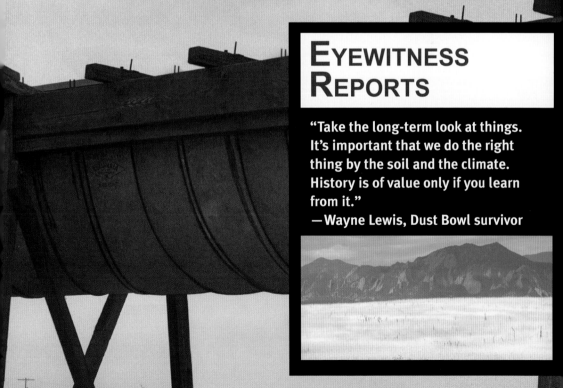

EYEWITNESS REPORTS

"Take the long-term look at things. It's important that we do the right thing by the soil and the climate. History is of value only if you learn from it."
—Wayne Lewis, Dust Bowl survivor

GLOSSARY

amenities (uh-MEH-nih-teez) *noun* things that make life easier (page 21)

bushel (BUH-shel) *noun* a unit of volume equal to about 20 kilograms (about 42 pounds) of flour or about 27 kilograms (about 60 pounds) of potatoes (page 6)

devastating (DEH-vuh-stay-ting) *adjective* causing severe damage (page 2)

drought (DROWT) *noun* a long period of dry weather (page 4)

grit (GRIT) *noun* small pieces of dirt or sand (page 14)

grueling (GROO-ling) *adjective* extremely difficult and exhausting (page 13)

optimism (AHP-tih-mih-zum) *noun* the feeling that everything will work out (page 8)

plains (PLANEZ) *noun* wide and flat expanses of land (page 2)

plight (PLITE) *noun* unfortunate condition (page 23)

reform (rih-FORM) *noun* improvement of a system (page 25)

refugees (REH-fyoo-jeez) *noun* people who escape from a specific place (page 21)

techniques (tek-NEEKS) *noun* methods of doing something, such as farming (page 10)

INDEX

ANALYZE THE TEXT

Use facts and details from the text to support your answers to the following questions.

- What was life like for people living in the Great Plains during the Dust Bowl?

- What events led to the mass migration of people from the Dust Bowl?

- How do the "Eyewitness Reports" increase your understanding of events described in the text?

- What role did Hugh H. Bennett play in helping the Great Plains recover from the Dust Bowl?

Comprehension:
Identify Cause and Effect

Use information from the text to list three causes that led up to the Dust Bowl.

Cause	Cause	Cause

Effect
the Dust Bowl